IMAGES OF ENGLAND

LONGTON

18 65
GREAT INDUSTRIA
LONGTON.
Ja-Ja
REGD
TRADE MARK.

IMAGES OF ENGLAND

LONGTON

DON HENSHALL

Frontispiece: Longton's coat of arms bears a Latin inscription which proclaims *Creat Industria*. This translates as 'let industry be brought to birth,' and can be seen here on this heraldic postcard. Unfortunately, the printer has made an error and the inscription reads *Great Industria*. The shield bears the motifs of the Edensor-Heathcotes, the Gresleys and the Sandfords, supported by a potter and a miner, complete with pick-axe. The spread-eagle crest is from the arms of James Glover, the first mayor of Longton, and includes the date of incorporation, 1865.

First published in 2007 by Tempus Publishing

Reprinted in 2008 by
The History Press
The Mill, Brimscombe Port,
Stroud, Gloucestershire, GL5 2QG
www.thehistorypress.co.uk

Reprinted 2013

British Library Cataloguing in Publication Data.
A catalogue record for this book is available from the British Library.

ISBN 978 0 7524 4499 4

Typesetting and origination by
Tempus Publishing.
Printed in Great Britain.

Contents

Acknowledgements   6

Introduction   7

one   Town Centre   9

two   Surrounding Area   19

three   Industry, Commerce and Transport   25

four   Religion   41

five   Education   57

six   People, Leisure and Entertainment   69

seven   Queen's Park   81

eight   Longton's Neighbours   95

Acknowledgements

In my efforts to produce this book I have been helped and encouraged by many people and, in particular, I would like to thank the following for their assistance in lending, finding or identifying material; without them the task would have been nigh on impossible:

Ellis Bevan; Peter and Grace Capper; the Churches Together In Longton, especially Father John Gilbert and the parish of St Gregory; Joan Dutton (née Bailey); Lewis Foreman; Harold Huson; Fred Hughes; David and Margaret Mycock of Abacus Books, Milton; Mohammed Nazir; Paul Pearson and John Cooke of the Potteries Omnibus Preservation Society; John and Sue Richardson; Eileen Rogan; Roger Simmons; Mrs Marie Simpson (Newbon), author of *This Potter's Clay – a History of St Gregory's Parish, Longton*; Glyn Thursfield; George Wass and Wm Williamson Ltd.

In addition, from my collection, I have been able to use a large number of reference books which have proved invaluable in checking and double-checking the factual information and dates. I thank the (often anonymous) compilers of these tomes.

In particular, I would recommend a book entitled *The History of Longton* by J.H.Y. Briggs, published by Keele University in 1982. This is a wonderful source of reference for an enquiring mind.

My family are getting used to the routine now and help in whichever way they can. A big thank you to Julie, Christie and Naomi.

Finally, my sincere thanks go to the staff at Tempus Publishing, in particular Cate, Beth and Laura. They are a pleasure to work with and are always so positive and supportive.

All reasonable steps have been taken to identify the owners of copyright of the images etc used in this book and unacknowledged copyright holders are welcome to contact us.

Introduction

Longton is not an old town in historical terms. It grew out of two small hamlets – the
hamlet of Longton, which existed in the area around Longton Hall, and Meare Lane
End a mile or so to the east. Records for 1666 show Longton to be much smaller than
the neighbouring villages of Burslem, Tunstall, Hanley and Stoke at that time.

Despite being situated on ancient routes – the Uttoxeter road dates back to Roman
times and the Stone road dates back to the thirteenth century – it was not until the
middle of the eighteenth century that the two villages began to develop and expand.
The main reason for this was that the main routes running through them to Uttoxeter,
Stone, Trentham and Adderley Green became turnpikes. This improved communications
and made the area an attractive location for new industry and it was around this time
that the manufacture of pottery began at Longton Hall when the area was found to
have an abundance of raw materials. Mining for coal and ironstone already existed and
supported a growing iron-smelting industry; so was now instrumental in supporting a
fledgling pottery industry as well.

A schoolroom was built at Lane End in 1760 and formal religion came to the area
with the building of the nearby St John's church in 1763. And so the foundations
were laid for the future well-being of the growing community. To complement this,
a Wesleyan Chapel opened in 1783 and a New Connexion chapel in 1797. By 1802
Longton is recorded as a market town and around this time the town as we know
it today was beginning to take shape as buildings, both public and commercial, were
erected along the main routes in and out of the town.

The name of Lane End began to wane during the first half of the nineteenth century
when it was considered a little derogatory. Some considered it to convey an idea of
meanness, which no longer applied to the new respectability of the place, and so Longton
was formally adopted as the name for the town in 1848 and Lane End disappeared from
use. I wonder if this could be the root of the local term 'Neck-end' for Longton? None
of the other explanations ever seemed appropriate and, strangely, none of the other six
towns have been afforded nicknames in the same way – offensive or otherwise.

During the nineteenth century the population grew rapidly, and from a mere 2,500
in 1780 it had grown to over 19,000 by 1871 as the number of potbanks grew to over
sixty-five in the same period and dominated the town. The area soon became flooded

A multi-view postcard of Longton.

with small factories turning out a variety of ceramic products and the skyline was a mass of bottle ovens of all shapes and sizes belching out their smoke.

Wedgwood never potted in Longton but many of the potters who did become established here were prominent in their own field of expertise and also became household names. One of the most famous was John Aynsley and some of the others were Webberley, Adderley, Beswick, T.C. Wild, Shelley, Sampson Bridgwood, Cartwright and Edwards, Goddard, Forrester, and so the list goes on. It would be virtually impossible to list all of the manufacturers of this period and, in a book this size, would leave no room for the illustrations, which are what really tell the story of Longton.

When the railway came to Longton in 1848 a station was built in an elevated position and an iron viaduct was constructed to carry the trains over the edge of Market Square (now Times Square). This has remained as an iconic symbol at the gateway of the town and features prominently on photographs and postcards over past generations.

More growth occurred in the earlier part of the twentieth century, but as the period drew to a close, the coal and pottery industries went into serious decline throughout North Staffordshire. Coal mines were closed and many of the pottery companies either ceased production or drastically restricted their operations when it became impossible to compete with foreign manufactured imports. In the absence of regional government assistance, the town began to change. This became more noticeable in Longton than elsewhere because of the smaller scale of the individual operations and their proximity to each other in and around the town centre.

Whatever the economic future holds for the town remains to be seen but, in the meantime, the pride of Longton lives on; its history has made the people what they are today and I hope this book will lift their spirits in a nostalgic celebration of yesteryear, remembering the people, places and events which helped put Longton on the map and make it truly great.

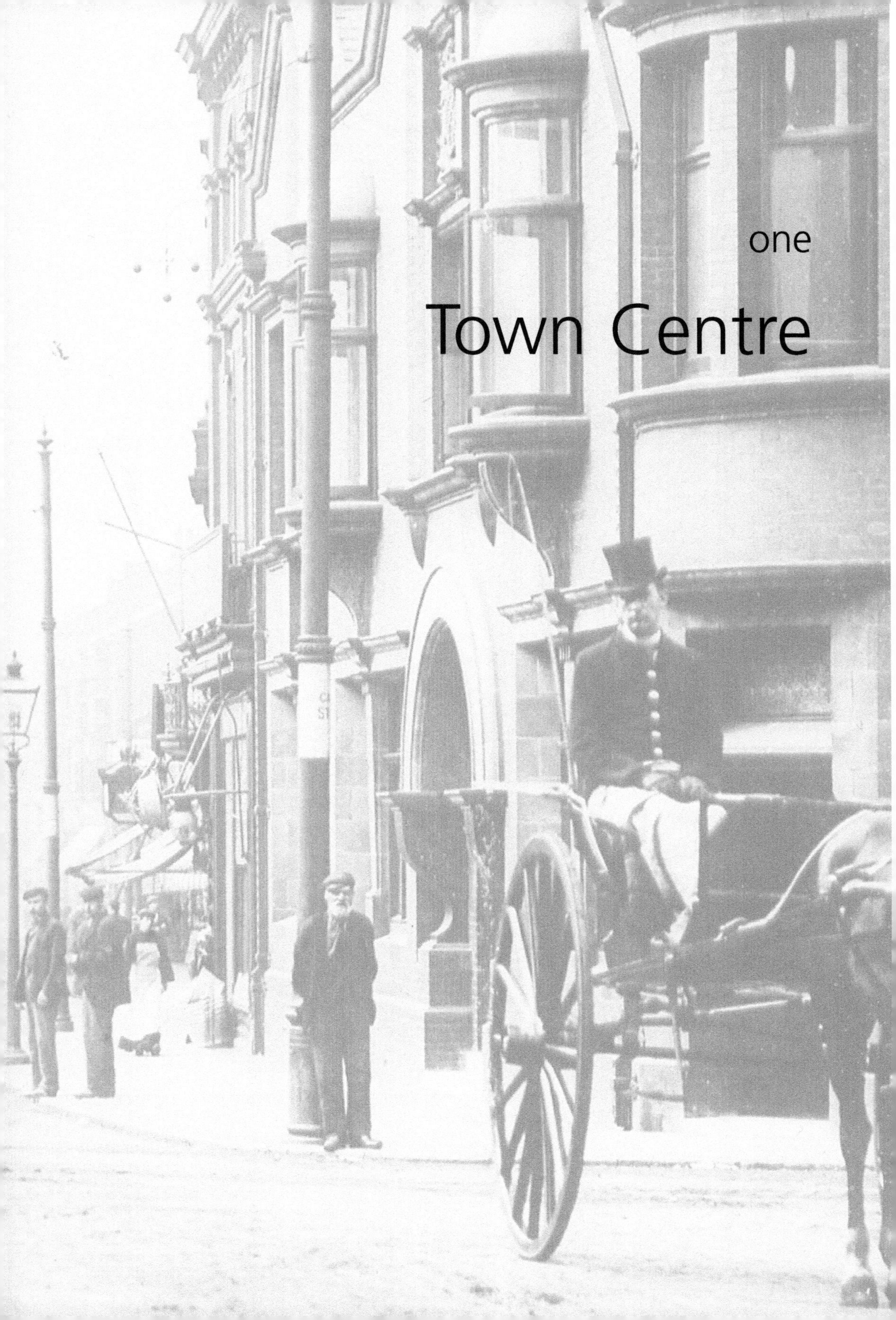
one
Town Centre

There have been many changes to the area since this aerial photograph was taken. Someone has dated it to 1930 but this is wrong since the parking bays of Longton's bus station can be seen at the bottom of the picture on the site of today's Bennett Precinct, yet this land was not acquired and developed until 1943. There are no other clear clues as to the exact date but, judging by the vehicles, it seems more likely for the picture to have been taken in the mid to late 1950s, especially as a series of

aerial photographs was taken across the city to celebrate the jubilee of Federation in 1960. In the middle right of the picture is St Gregory's Pugin-designed Gothic church. The area above this is now part of Tesco's car park. At the top centre can be seen Cooke Street/Edensor C. of E. Junior and Infants School and below this, in the middle of the picture, is Beswick's factory where today's latest retail development has been built. Many of the shops lining The Strand are still trading today.

Mr Stephen A. Hughes and Mr Arthur Landon Harber began their partnership as stationers and printers on 31 March 1888, trading from premises in Boardman Buildings, Stafford Street. The business was known for its high standard of workmanship and the dedication of its staff and it developed and grew. However, two years after starting, Mr Hughes died on Christmas Day 1890, but Mr Harber continued to trade under both names and the business flourished. In 1897 new purpose built premises were opened at No. 51 Market Street, and in the same

year the business was appointed printer by Royal Warrant to His Royal Highness, the Prince of Wales, and became known as the Royal Press. In 1906 Mr A.L. Harber was appointed mayor of Longton and, in the following year, the business was appointed printers and publishers to His Majesty the King. Hughes & Harber produced a *Longton Trade Directory and Year Book* from 1890 to 1913 and produced high quality commercial and private work for a number of prestigious clients including various Freemasonry Lodges and the Staffordshire Province of Freemasons. In 1971 the Longton premises closed and the business amalgamated with J.G. Fenn Ltd. This view is from a postcard sent in 1904 and clearly shows the Royal Crest above the shop entrance. Today the building is occupied by insurance brokers.

An early view of Market Street at the corner of Commerce Street, postmarked 1906. The business to the left is Charles Wilson Boast, ironmongers.

Market Street looking towards Times Square appears rather busy in this 1907 view. In the distance, in the middle of the picture, is the railway viaduct and to the right is the Heathcote Arms. One of the shops beyond the public house is a pawnbroker and the traditional three-ball sign can be seen above the shop silhouetted against the sky. The carriage with the liveried driver seems to be waiting for a rather important person. N.B. The spidery starshape in the centre of the picture has been drawn by the sender of this postcard to indicate the location of the station.

The Heathcote family lived at Longton Hall from 1777 and were prominent landowners. The Heathcote Arms in Market Street, at the corner of Anchor Road, was a substantial property and reflects the importance of the family name in Longton.

This impressive view, showing the side elevation in Anchor Road, gives an indication of the overall size of the Heathcote Arms. The public house no longer exists and has been replaced by a bland modern building which currently lies empty awaiting a new tenant.

By the 1920s McKnight's clothiers had taken over the premises of Boast's Ironmongers at the junction of Market Street and Commerce Street. Frank Flint's shop, selling wines and spirits (at the extreme right of this picture) was trading at No. 71 Market Street and, a few doors away, at No. 63, was John Thorley's drapery shop.

Here is a busy scene in Market Street, *c.* 1950. The view shows the lower end of the street, below the Anchor Road junction, and beyond the Heathcote Arms, towards the railway bridge.

The photographer who took this photograph must have been standing in the middle of Commerce Street looking towards Market Street. To his right is the Old Court House which dates from 1814. It earlier served as the Union Market Hall and the Old Town Hall and was finally demolished in 1950 to be replaced by a small public garden.

This view of Stafford Street (now The Strand) gives a clear view of the Wesleyan Chapel where the Methodist Central Hall stands today. The shop on the right, where the two men are standing, is Bradley's Pawnbrokers and the familiar three-ball sign can be seen clearly outlined against the sky above the shop.

The town's indoor market was built in 1863, and is clearly visible to the right of this picture taken in Stafford Street in the 1950s. This market is unusual, if not unique in the Potteries, insofar as some of the shops on Stafford Street can be accessed directly from within the Market Hall.

Standing around in Market Place (now Times Square) would not have been recommended with trams criss-crossing the area during the 1920s. This was, and still is, a busy junction at the gateway to the town. The railway viaduct is to the left and the eye is drawn straight ahead into Market Street. To the right is the Town Hall which was built in 1863.

Still in Market Place, and turning fully round to look in the opposite direction into Stafford Street, we see a group of men who appear to be waiting for the bar to open at the Eagle public house on the corner. Next door to the pub, at No. 4, is Edwin Adams' hat and hosiery shop. At No. 6, Mrs Anne Poulson trades as a confectioner. Number 8 Stafford Street is the shop of Amies Ltd, boot makers, and No. 10 is Barclay's bank. The prominent building to the left of centre, with the conical tower, is Boardman Buildings which housed a number of retail establishments. In this picture from around 1910, the main business in the building is that of Richard Amor, draper. By 1912, the premises had been taken over by William Baker's tailoring business.

This early 1950s view of Market Place – here called Town Hall Square – (and later renamed Times Square) is taken from the elevated railway station and shows a single-deck bus negotiating the roundabout in front of the Town Hall. A banner fastened to the front of the Town Hall advises passers-by to 'Keep On Saving.'

Two trams pass under the railway bridge in this 1905 picture. Steam rises from a train about to cross the bridge and in the foreground a group of men stand around chatting. Behind the bridge, to the right is the Crown and Anchor Hotel and to its left is the now-demolished church of St John. At the top of the pillar supporting the bridge can be seen the town's coat of arms carved in the stone.

A similar view, from an elevated position, shows a North Staffordshire Railway engine about to leave the station and cross the bridge whilst men and women go about their daily business on the road below.

This view from outside St John's church, alongside the Crown and Anchor Hotel looks down on a bus bearing the registration number VT-6211. This vehicle was acquired new in 1931 by M.E. Allen & Sons, an independent bus operator in Sneyd Green, which also traded under the name of Greyhound Motors. Allen's had a small fleet of buses and this one is No. 4. The bus transferred to PMT in 1935 to become No. 250 in their fleet, and it was eventually sold to Stevenson's of Uttoxeter in 1938, before being finally scrapped in 1944. The bus in the background, just passing the Town Hall entrance, was operated by Lymer's on the Longton–Hilderstone route.

two

Surrounding Area

Above: In 1868, the original Cottage Hospital was opened in Mount Pleasant (now Lawley Street). It moved to a new site on the same street in 1879 and was eventually replaced by the current hospital in 1889-90 on land at Upper Belgrave Road. John Aynsley JP (1823-1907), who served as mayor of Longton for four successive years from 1886, was able to persuade the Duke of Sutherland to give land for the new hospital and he was innovative in raising funds for the hospital for many years after. This view dates from 1902.

Right: This message is written on the back of a postcard which bears a totally unrelated view. It was published by Raphael Tuck & Sons, one of the largest producers of postcards at the beginning of the twentieth century, and posted in 1906. The text reads: 'Please help the Longton Cottage Hospital, Longton by buying a packet of six Tuck's Postcards and contribute to the Postcard Chain for the above hospital to help it to £1,000 and £50 for yourself. Post the cards according to Rules supplied free by all

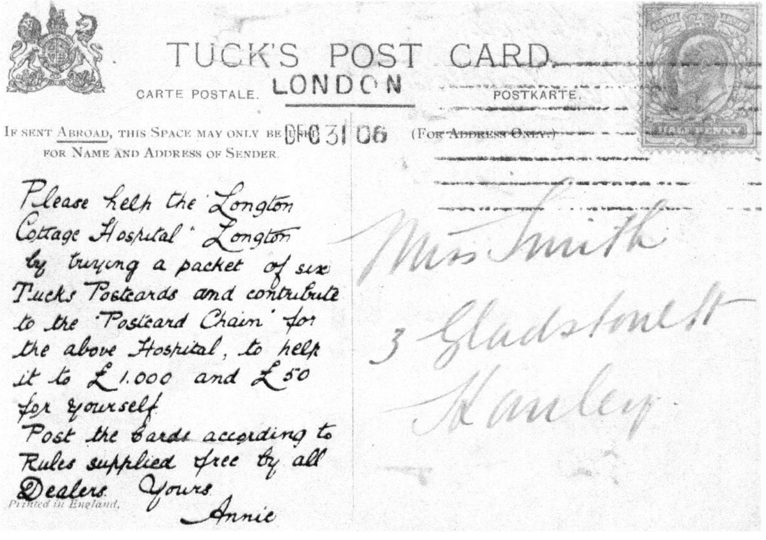

Dealers. Yours, Annie.' Could this have been one of John Aynsley's fund-raising ideas, and did anyone locally win the £50 prize? Answers on the back of a postcard please!

An almost deserted Chaplin Road, *c.* 1917. Could it be a Sunday as the blinds are down on Hawley & Sherwins' grocers shop on the corner of Hamilton Road, and the family on the right, dressed in their best clothes, look as if they are on their way to church or chapel?

Somehow, on this normally quiet and peaceful Chaplin Road, on a bright summer's day in around 1960, an Austin A40 car met a PMT bus in a spectacular smash. The two vehicles ended up fully on the pavement on opposite sides of the wide road. Garden walls have been demolished, a tree has been partially uprooted and both vehicles are extensively damaged. The bobbies are on the scene to control the crowds which have gathered around each vehicle, but there is no sign of any casualties. Did everyone get out safely, and did Chaplin Road once again return to normality? Let's hope so.

Much of the Florence and Dresden area of Longton is built on what was once the Duke of Sutherland's estate and many streets bear names associated with his family. For many years the Duke remained the area's largest landowner and landlord and he served as mayor of Longton in 1895-6. He gave land in Lightwood Road (formerly Stone Road) for the building of the Sutherland Institute, and the foundation stone was laid by King Edward VII, then the Prince of Wales, in January 1897. The completed building was opened in 1899 and the ground floor housed the town's library (removed from the Town Hall). On the upper floors were a Science and Art School. This view of the imposing building was taken soon after it opened in around 1900.

A view of Trentham Road, Dresden looking towards Trentham with tram lines running along the centre of the road and a number of pedestrians going about their business.

From the window panes of the large bay of this house (No. 64 Trentham Road), it is clear that it belonged to the Misses Hood, who were milliners. The 1912 edition of *Kelly's Directory* for Staffordshire shows this business being run by Gertrude and Millicent Hood. By 1928, Gertrude was trading on her own.

This view, taken from the tower of St James' church on Uttoxeter Road, is of East Vale. The area lies to the north of the North Staffordshire Railway line and east of Anchor Road which leads to Adderley Green. By the late 1870s much of Goddard Street and Ford Street had been built up with terraced housing.

Industry, Commerce and Transport

An 1865 advert for William Webberley's 'improved china'. Having started out working for Minton's, Webberley left and formed a partnership with G. Shubotham in 1841-42. They originally made lustreware but then concentrated on china production. After Shubotham's death in 1847 Webberley continued on his own and he rebuilt the factory in 1888. He became chief bailiff of Longton in 1857-8, 1859-60 and 1861-2, and was an active Magistrate. Webberley died in 1892, aged seventy-six and is buried in St James's churchyard. Despite the wide variety of products here advertised by W.J. Salt, little is recorded about the company.

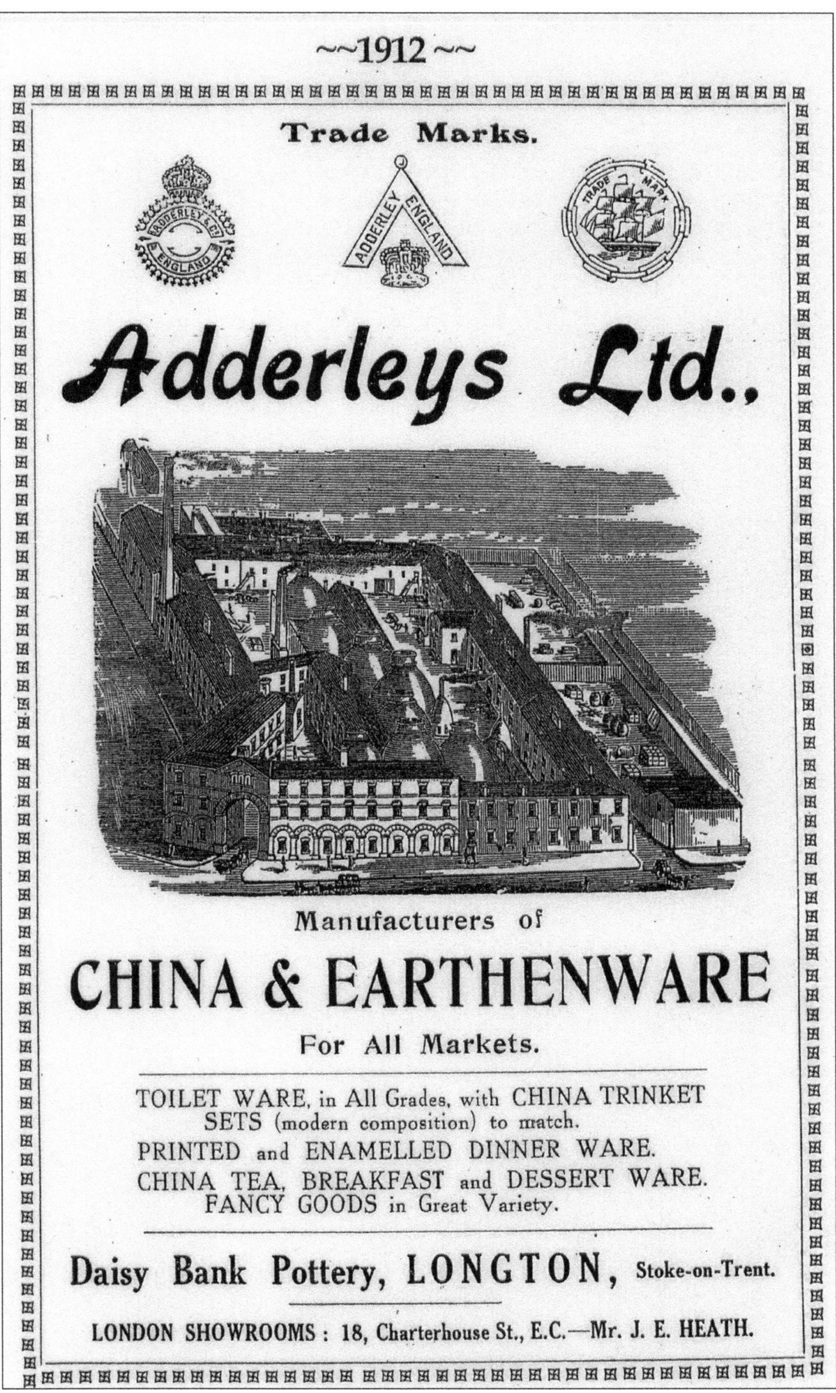

William Alsager Adderley took on the sole ownership of the Daisy Bank works in Spring Garden Road, following the death of his partners Nixon, in 1869, and Hulse in 1874 and continued to manufacture an extensive variety of china and earthenware products until 1905 when the business began to trade as Adderley's Ltd, becoming a subsidiary of Ridgway Potteries. The factory was later renamed as the Gainsborough Works.

Right: Aynsley is one of the best-known names in the Staffordshire Potteries. Its history dates back to the turn of the nineteenth century when John Aynsley moved to the Potteries from his native Northumberland. He is believed to be Longton's first manufacturer of lustreware. When the family's circumstances were reduced around 1830, grandson John Aynsley first attended a dame school and then began working for various employers from the age of nine. He eventually moved out of the Potteries only to return some years later when he became a partner to Sampson Bridgwood. In 1861 John Aynsley built the Portland Works in Sutherland Road. As a prominent person in Longton, John Aynsley went on to be the town's mayor for four successive years from 1886 and was instrumental in the creation of Longton Park where a memorial clock tower was erected in his memory. Both the present Queen and the late Diana, Princess of Wales, chose Aynsley dinner services as their wedding gifts from the British pottery industry.

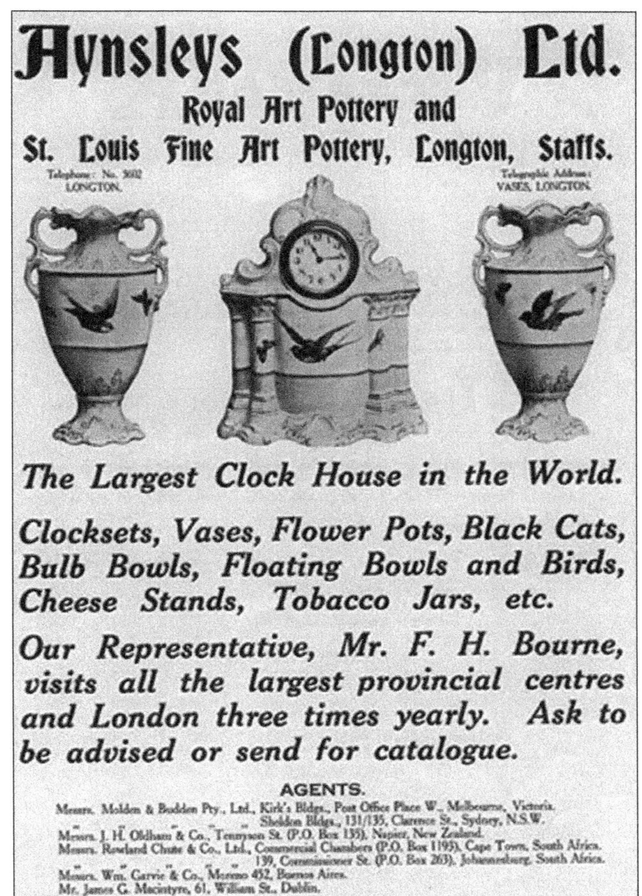

Opposite: James Wright Beswick (1845–1920) was born in Tunstall where his father Robert, was something of an entrepreneur. Robert started out as a joiner and builder and, by 1851, had an earthenware factory at Church Bank Works, a coal and ironstone mine at Great Chell and had manufactured bricks and tiles at Dale Hall, Burslem. He was also a member of the Tunstall Local Board of Health and chief bailiff in 1864.

It was no small wonder then that his son, James, followed in his father's footsteps and began potting himself. His first works were at Albion Street, Longton, in around 1890, then he moved to Britannia Works, High Street and finally to Gold Street *c.* 1899. Like his father, James was involved in local politics and was elected to Longton Borough Council. He also served Stoke-upon-Trent Borough Council and represented Kidsgrove on Staffordshire County Council. James was also a prominent member of the Methodist congregation on Stone Road and yet still found time to play bowls for Florence Bowling Club! This 1912 advert describes all kinds of earthenware and china products and the ware is still very collectable today. The company remained in the family's hands after James' death and became famous towards the middle of the twentieth century for its manufacture of ceramic animals of all kinds. Royal Doulton acquired the firm in 1969 but, by 2002, production of the Beswick range had ceased. The Gold Street works were demolished in 2003–4 to make way for a new retail development. There has always been confusion over the pronunciation of the Beswick name. English grammar might dictate that the word is pronounced 'Bezz-ick' – but most Potteries folk would know it as 'Bezz-wick' and would be quick to correct any mispronunciation!

The Co-operative Wholesale Society Ltd created its crockery department by taking over an existing manufactory on King Street, Longton, in the late 1940s, trading under the names of Clarence China and Windsor China. This impressive letterhead shows an engraving of the factory premises.

GEO. W. HARKER

Art Photographer and High-class Picture Framer

63, Market St., LONGTON

Specialities:

Children's Portraits. - Enlargements in all Processes. Permanent Carbon Miniatures on Ivory, artistically finished in Water Colours.

COPIES.

Copies from old or faded originals. Special care and attention is paid to this particular branch of photography, and customers may rely on a faithful reproduction from treasured photograph entrusted to me, without any alteration or damage whatever to the original. Quotations per return for Copy orders by post.

Longton had a large number of independent photographers and picture framers. In 1911, George W. Harker was trading from No. 63 Market Street but by 1928 the premises had been taken over by a clothier's business and there is no mention of what happened to Mr Harker or his business.

Left: The business of Wagstaff & Brunt seems to have concentrated mainly on commemorative wares between 1880 and 1927, especially Jubilee pieces in 1897. However, in later years, Messrs C.M. Brunt Jnr and W. Waterfield trading as Wagstaff & Brunt specialised in hotelware and glassware. In this 1940s advert the company is proudly proclaiming the benefits of their Adamtine Institutional ware. Apparently it is 'supreme in its clean appearance and hardness and extremely economic in price and service,' and, its 'surface does not craze so is ideally hygienic as a non-carrier of infection'.

Below: This advertising headline perfectly describes the business in a few words. The shop occupied a prestigious site in the Boardman Buildings in Stafford Street and the following pictures are taken from a full-page advert in the 1911 publication *Staffordshire Past and Present by Pen and Camera.* The book is described as 'an historical pictorial and descriptive guide'.

In the ladies' department, this advert shows the latest 'Paris Models made by our own tailors'.

Further ladies' garments are displayed around the shop on mannequins and carefully placed cards pronounce the existence of 'Practical Skilled Cutters'.

In the men's department a glass cabinet at the foot of the ornate staircase displays fine examples of ties, cravats and braces. A nearby card states 'Goods Exhibited and Sold made from Best Selected Wool'.

Cutters hard at work in the men's department preparing tailored suits.

James Myott & Sons' Bon Marché draper's shop occupied a prominent position at Nos 23 and 25 Market Street, on the corner of Railway Passage, and this atmospheric picture shows a wonderful range of goods for sale in their windows.

Left: Mr Clewlow, the coalman from Leveson Street, does not look as if he's out delivering nutty slack today does he?

Opposite: This 1893 advert shows how national companies were opening branches in provincial towns. Locally, the Singer Manufacturing Company had shops in Hanley, Newcastle, Longton and Tunstall and the Longton shop was managed by Charles Greaves. A Singer shop is still trading in Market Street, Longton 114 years later.

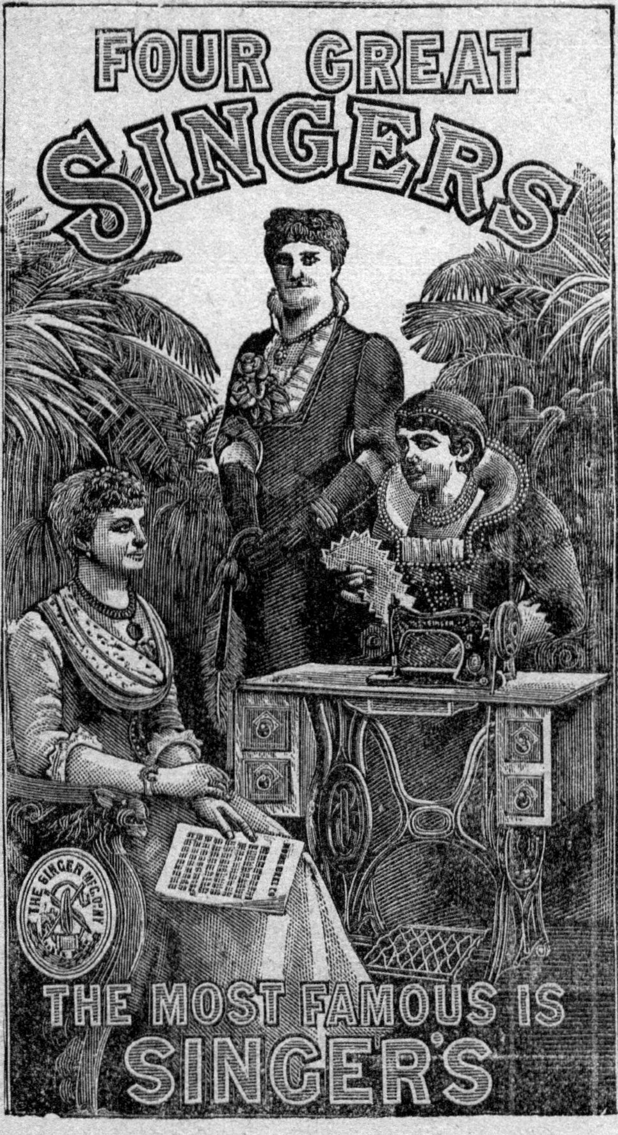

SEWING MACHINE

LOCAL SHOW ROOMS :—

35, Piccadilly, HANLEY.

1a, Red Lion Square, NEWCASTLE.

17, Market Street, LONGTON.

New Town Hall, TUNSTALL.

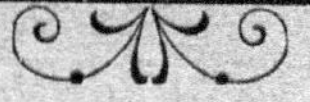

These men aren't off to work either by the looks of it. In fact, this photograph shows the Wass's horses dressed for a May Day parade *c.* 1920. Former Lord Mayor Bill Wass recalled that everybody used horses in those days and T.C. Wild's even had nine horses of their own. Bill Wass is standing on the extreme right of this picture holding one of the horses and his father (Bill Snr) is sitting at the front of the cart on the left, with his arms folded.

This Harmil delivery van belonged to Harry Mills, grocer, of Nos 15 and 17 Uttoxeter Road and is parked outside No. 79 Buccleuch Road. The driver is William Edward Taylor, born 1898, who was later to work at Swynnerton armaments factory. The boys are his sons Reginald Rainforth Taylor, born 1923 and Don William Taylor born 1928, and the photograph was taken in around 1930.

Right: The first porcelain works to start manufacturing in the town began at Longton Hall in 1750. The factory was set up by William Jenkinson, who was joined in the venture by William Littler of Hanley. The business only lasted until 1760 and, consequently, examples of the ware are quite rare today. On this postcard is an example of a plate with a brilliant blue border which is on display in a London museum.

Below: Some more examples of Longton Hall pottery (*c.* 1754) on display at the Potteries Museum in Hanley.

'A Bird's Eye View of the Potteries at Longton' is the title on this postcard. The view is from the top of St James's church tower, with Uttoxeter Road to the left and looks ahead towards Meir.

Another view from St James's tower, this time looking towards Dresden. Hudson & Middleton's factory is at the bottom left, and in the middle of the picture, to the right, is St James's School. Beyond it lies the Phoenix Laundry and the Sutherland Institute.

Florence Colliery dates from 1874 and was named after the 3rd Duke of Sutherland's eldest daughter. This pit became one of the most modern in the area and underwent large scale development in NCB days. It was merged with the Hem Heath Colliery at nearby Trentham in 1974. The last coal drawn from Florence Pit was in 1981 and the site closed completely in 1992. The whole area has since been cleared and new housing and a school have been built there in recent years. The engine *Terrible* was in use at Florence Pit.

The pits throughout the North Staffordshire coalfield were provided with contracted public transport to convey the miners to and from their places of work. Here is one of the PMT buses, which was brought into service in 1949. In the 1950s and '60s it was not uncommon to see groups of miners waiting at bus stops with their towels under their arms and 'snapping' bags slung on their shoulders waiting for the colliery bus to collect them.

'The old and the new.' Well, they were in 1926 when bus EH7902 was acquired to replace tram No. 82. The bus was operated by the Potteries Electric Traction Co. (to be known as Potteries Motor Traction Co. Ltd from May 1933) until 1935, when it was withdrawn from service and sold to Lewis (Breakers) of Hanley. The first electric tramway in the Potteries was opened on 16 May 1899, and the tram in this picture was purchased from the makers, Midland Carriage and Wagon Co. and put into service in 1900/01. After various alterations and rebuilds, tram No. 82 was sold to Wemyss & District Tramways in 1928 and ran until 1933.

four
Religion

The parish of St James the Less was formed at Longton in 1834. The church, erected in 1833, to a design by James Trubshaw (architect of St Peter's, Stoke), was consecrated on 20 June 1834 by Bishop Ryder. An organ was installed in 1878. Several renovations took place over the ensuing years, together with much restoration work. The building is quite an imposing structure and is visible from much of the surrounding area.

An interior view of St James's church.

Left: This view shows the scale of the building from nearby School Lane (now Webberley Lane). The photograph is taken at its junction with Sheaf Passage, and in the distance the gates of the church can be seen, on Normacot Road. Uttoxeter Road lies to the far side of the church.

Below: The Lane End church of St John the Baptist stood to the north of Times Square alongside the Crown and Anchor Hotel. The church was begun in 1763 and completed and consecrated in 1764. It was rebuilt on the same site in 1792, enlarged in 1827-8 and restored in 1889. It no longer exists, having been demolished in 1979, but its memory lives on in old photographs and postcards. This view dates from 1903.

The building of Longton's first Catholic church was started in 1819 and it was finished in 1820. The church was erected on a piece of land known as Brick House Fields, between the present Gregory Street and Griffin Street. The adjoining presbytery was completed in 1835. The church was dedicated to St Gregory the Great and the first resident priest was Father Edward Daniel.

With the rapidly increasing Catholic population in Longton, it became obvious that a much larger church was required and Bishop Ullathorne repeatedly encouraged a later parish priest, Father James Massam, to consider building one, and this was the result of their efforts. This picture shows the 'new' St Gregory's which was opened on 20 July 1869 in Heathcote Road. This building, in the Gothic style, was of cathedral proportions and the architect was Edward Pugin, son of the celebrated Augustus Welby Pugin.

Here are three Catholic priests of St Gregory's pictured in 1912. On the left is Revd Bernard J. McQuirk (curate at Longton 1911-12); on the right is Revd Samuel Myerscough (curate 1912-16), and in the centre Revd John Stringfellow, (parish priest and rector from 1882-1917).

Another photograph of Revd John Stringfellow and Revd Bernard McQuirk, *c.* 1911-12.

The Sacred Heart Altar, 1912.

Our Lady's Altar, 1912.

Opposite: The magnificent High Altar of the Pugin church, 1912.

Above: Another of the Catholic priests from St Gregory's but, unfortunately, he remains unidentified.

Opposite above, left and right: The pulpit and the pietà, 1912.

Opposite below: Two more priests from St Gregory's pose for a formal photograph with a number of men from the parish – but who are they?

Above left: A picture of Revd William Walsh, parish priest 1934-1953, taken at the time of his silver jubilee in 1942.

Above right: Revd Francis Gallagher, curate to Father Walsh and Father O'Connor, 1953-56.

Left: Revd Donal O'Connor, parish priest 1953-63.

Opposite: This picture is taken from a painting of the nave by local artist Reginald Haggar (1905-1988). It was commissioned in 1953 by the newly-appointed parish priest, Father Donal O'Connor.

REGINALD G. HAGGAR

'More tea, Fathers?' Curates Revd Edward Motherway, Revd John McCarthy and Revd Norman Millard with parish priest Revd Donal O'Connor *c*. 1957.

Left: Parish priest Revd Desmond Donnelly (1964-1991), and his newly-appointed curate Revd Terence Luxon (1968-72) in 1968.

Opposite below: With spiralling costs and further repairs needed, the decision was duly taken to demolish the church and presbytery. This picture taken in 1968 shows the work in progress.

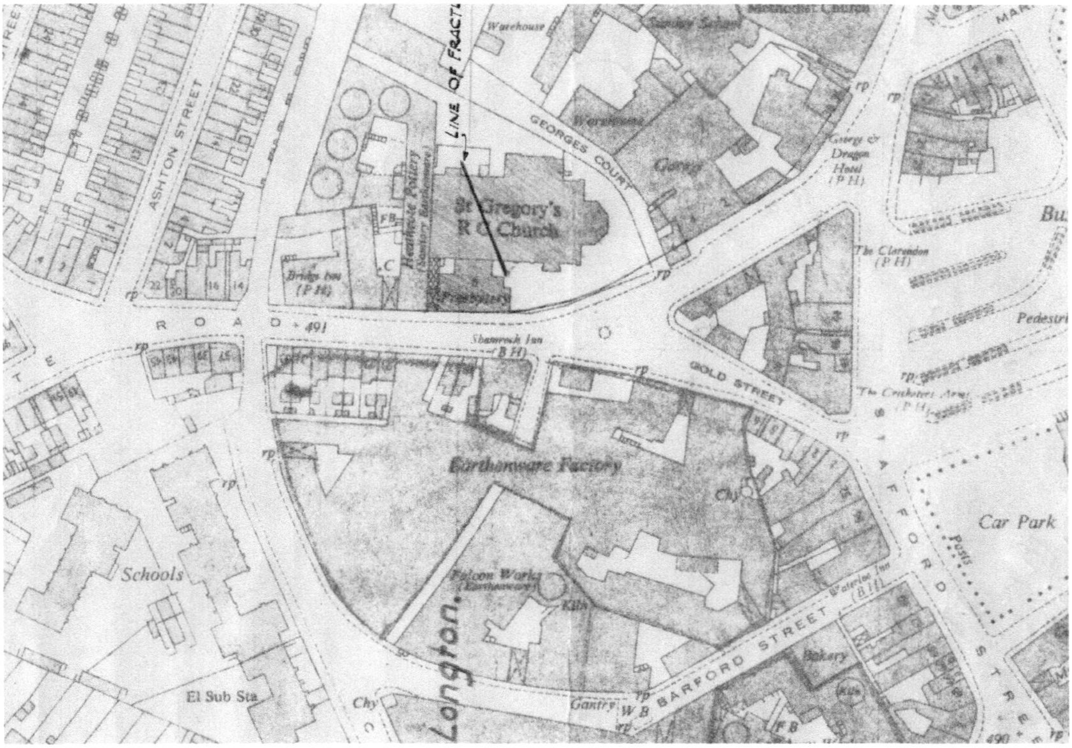

Above: This map of Longton shows St Gregory's church in the centre with a dark line running diagonally through it. This was the identified fault line which was to lead to its ultimate closure. By 1960 mining subsidence had greatly affected the church and presbytery in Heathcote Street and £35,000 was needed to carry out the repairs. In addition, a further £20,000 was required to restore the crumbling parish hall in Gregory Street.

Above: The church is reduced to a mere shell. Many of the artefacts from the church were salvaged before demolition and donated to parishioners.

Below: This evocative picture shows the remains of the beautiful Pugin decoration around the High Altar whilst six teenagers idly rummage around the site.

Right: Almost gone!

Below: The responsibility for demolishing the old church and building a new one in its place on the same site had fallen, soon after his appointment, to the new parish priest, Revd Desmond Donnelly (1964-91) and a radical design for the new St Gregory's emerged.

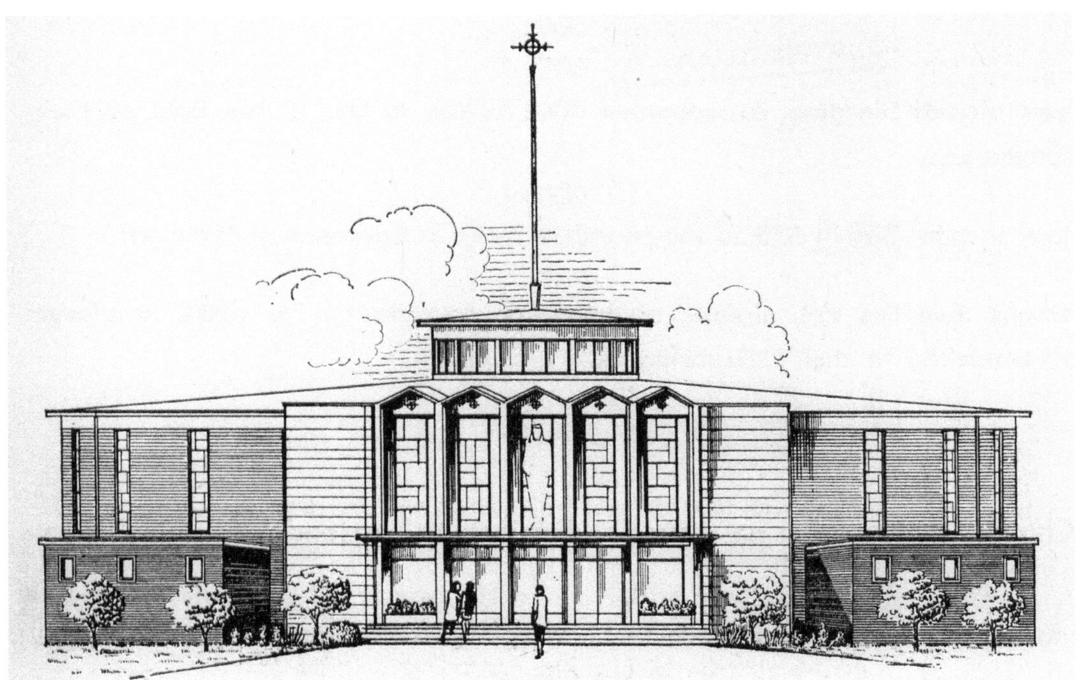

There was much under-pinning of the foundations required to ensure no repetition of the previous subsidence problem – 150 tons of concrete were used to make the ground safe again. Here we see the steelwork frame bolted in place as the new church takes shape.

five
Education

Florence School on Lilleshall Street, founded in 1886 as a boys', girls' and infants' school. This picture, taken in 2007, shows the closed and boarded-up school awaiting demolition.

This 2007 photograph shows the pediment above the entrance to Florence School which incorporates an elaborate stone carving of the town's coat of arms. Beneath this is further carving depicting a banner which originally bore the name 'Florence Schools' and confirmed the date of building as 1885. At some time and for some completely unknown and mysterious reason, the name 'Florence' was chiselled away and completely obliterated, leaving just the word 'Schools' remaining.

Above: A picture of children at Florence Infants in around 1936, dancing around the Maypole – Francis Bailey is the third boy from the right.

Below: In this long-exposure photograph (*c.* 1950) there seems to have been a bit of fidgeting going on in this class of forty-one children at Florence School as some of the faces appear blurred.

This 1937 photograph taken at Cooke Street School, Edensor, shows the nursery class about to have their lunch.

Longton High School was built on land acquired at Trentham Road in 1885 to accommodate 200 boys. After numbers began to fall in the 1890s a radical reassessment enabled it to run as a mixed school which had dramatic results and rapidly increased its numbers. By 1940 it was necessary to move to larger premises at Sandon Road which could not be fully occupied until 1947 due to the intervention of the war.

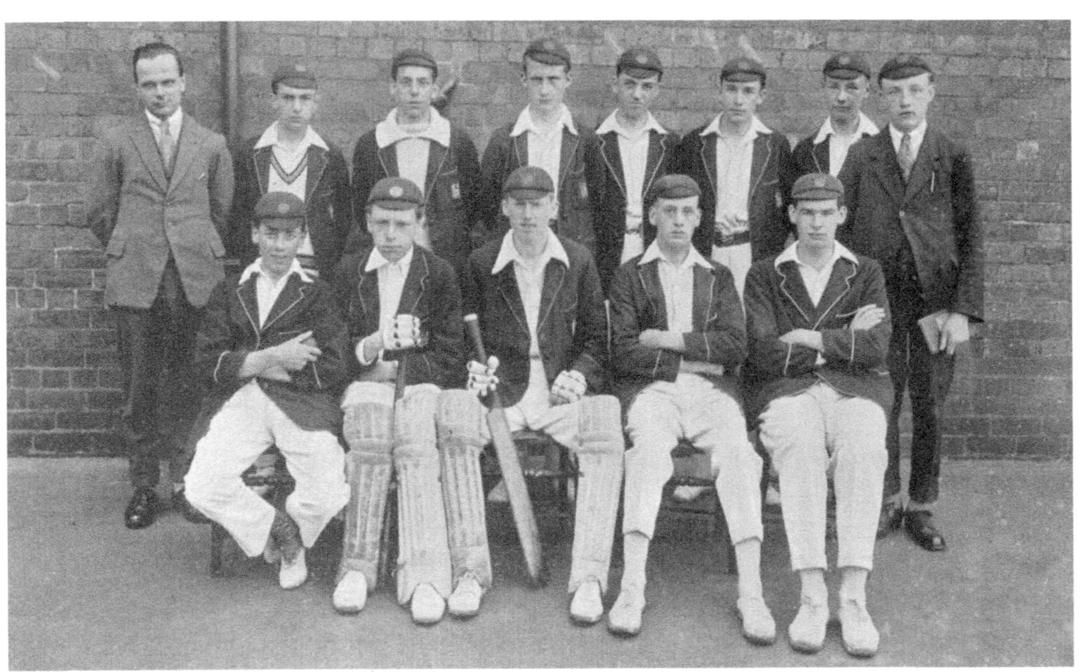

Longton High School cricket team, 1925.

St Gregory's old school buildings were built on Gregory Street in 1820 and, by the late 1880s, had been condemned by the local education department. New schools were commissioned which would accommodate 'boys', girls' and infants' departments' and the first phase, the boys' school, was opened on a new site at Cemetery Road by Bishop Ilsley, on Wednesday 24 July 1889. The cost of this was £1,400, of which £1,200 had been subscribed and paid by the parishioners. Bishop Ilsley's first appointment as a curate following his ordination in 1861 was at Longton, where he served the parish for twelve years alongside Revd James Massam, parish priest. During this time Father Ilsley saw the acquisition of the land at Heathcote Road and the building of the magnificent Pugin church of St Gregory, which was opened on 20 July 1869. He was consecrated as a bishop in 1879 and appointed to Birmingham Diocese on 17 February 1888.

The note with this St Gregory's photograph dates it to 1907 and shows a class of girls in their pinafores and medals apparently having just received their first Holy Communion.

Father Donal O'Connor sits amongst over seventy children celebrating their first Holy Communion in the mid-1950s. The girls are dressed in white dresses and veils, whilst the boys wear a traditional sash.

George Arthur Mitcheson (1868-1934) was a prominent mining engineer in Longton, following in his father's and grandfather's footsteps. At various times he managed many of the area's collieries, including Meir Hay, Stafford Iron & Coal, and Florence. He was also mining engineer at Berry Hill and a director of Mossfield Collieries. He was a pioneer of many mining improvements and much respected in his field. In 1903 the Mitcheson Swimming Shield was introduced and, along with other schools in the town, St Gregory's pupils were invited to compete. Not only did they win it in the first year but they went on to win it for the next twenty-five years, after which it was deemed to be the property of the school! This picture appears on a commemorative postcard issued after the first 'ten successful years' in 1913.

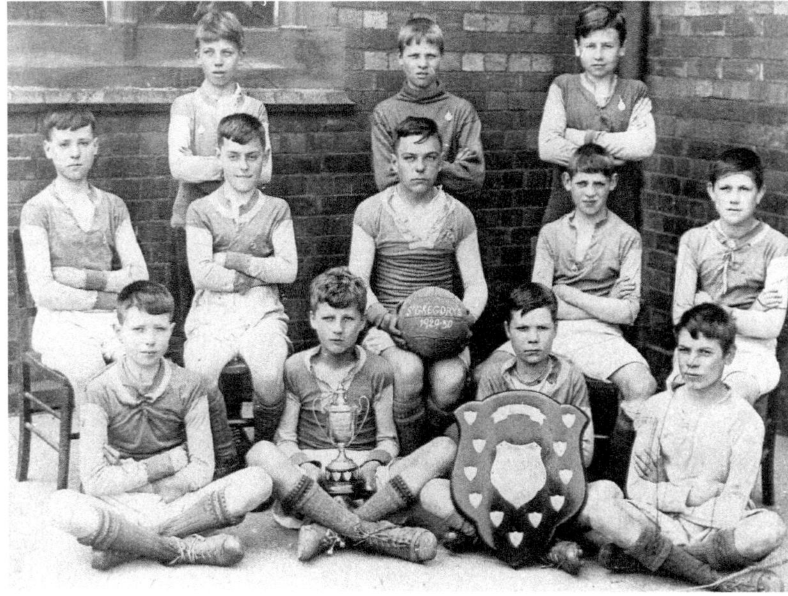

St Gregory's RC football team – Schools Champions 1929-30.

St Gregory's RC Schools Champions again in 1939-40. The teachers are Vincent Coppinger on the left and Joe Day on the right. Stanley Whitfield is standing to the left of the goalkeeper.

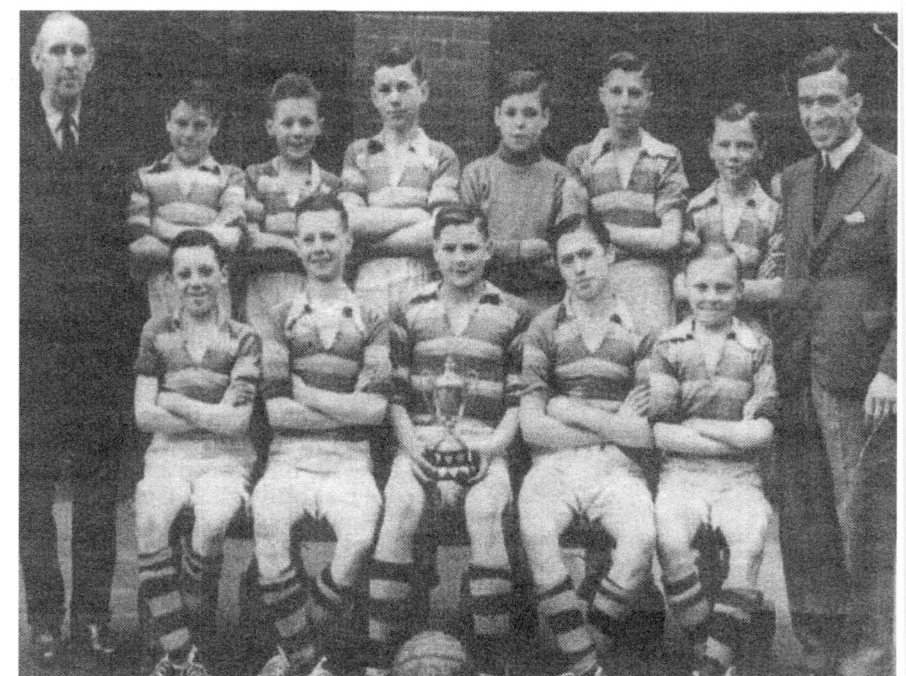

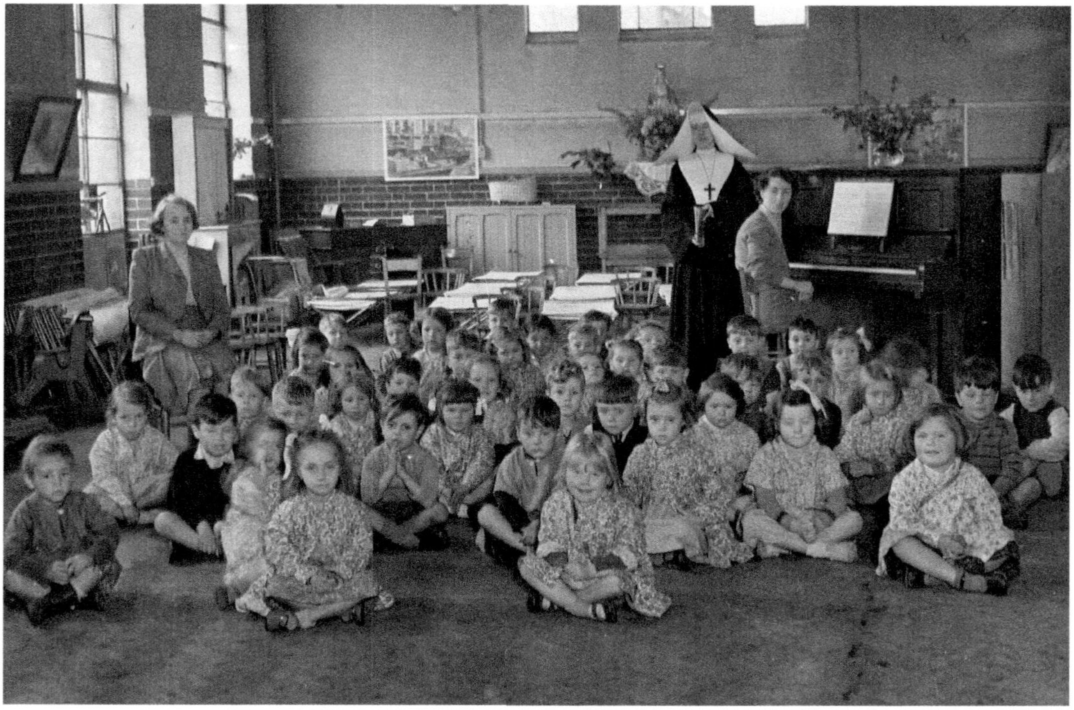

St Gregory's Nursery pictured in 1950. The teacher on the left is Mrs Winifred Meakin. Sister Marie, head of the Infant's Dept, is standing next to Kath Dooley, who is seated at the piano.

In 1952, St Gregory's had five sets of twins. Can you tell them apart?

St Gregory's Christmas party, 1952.

St Gregory's Christmas party 1954. Fathers O'Connor and Gallagher are resplendent in their paper hats!

St Gregory's female staff, 1954. Standing (left to right): -?-, Mrs Molly O'Brien (née Lilley), Mrs Molly Margaret Rowley (née Loftus), Miss Kath Dooley, -?-. Seated (left to right): Miss Winnie O'Connor, Sister Marie, Mrs Winnie Meakin.

St Gregory's staff picture. Back row (left to right): -?-, Glendora Lee, Mrs Howard (née Day), -?-. Front row (left to right): Miss Dolly Kane, Joe Patton, Sister Berchmans, Gerald Capper, Miss Adelaide Beardmore.

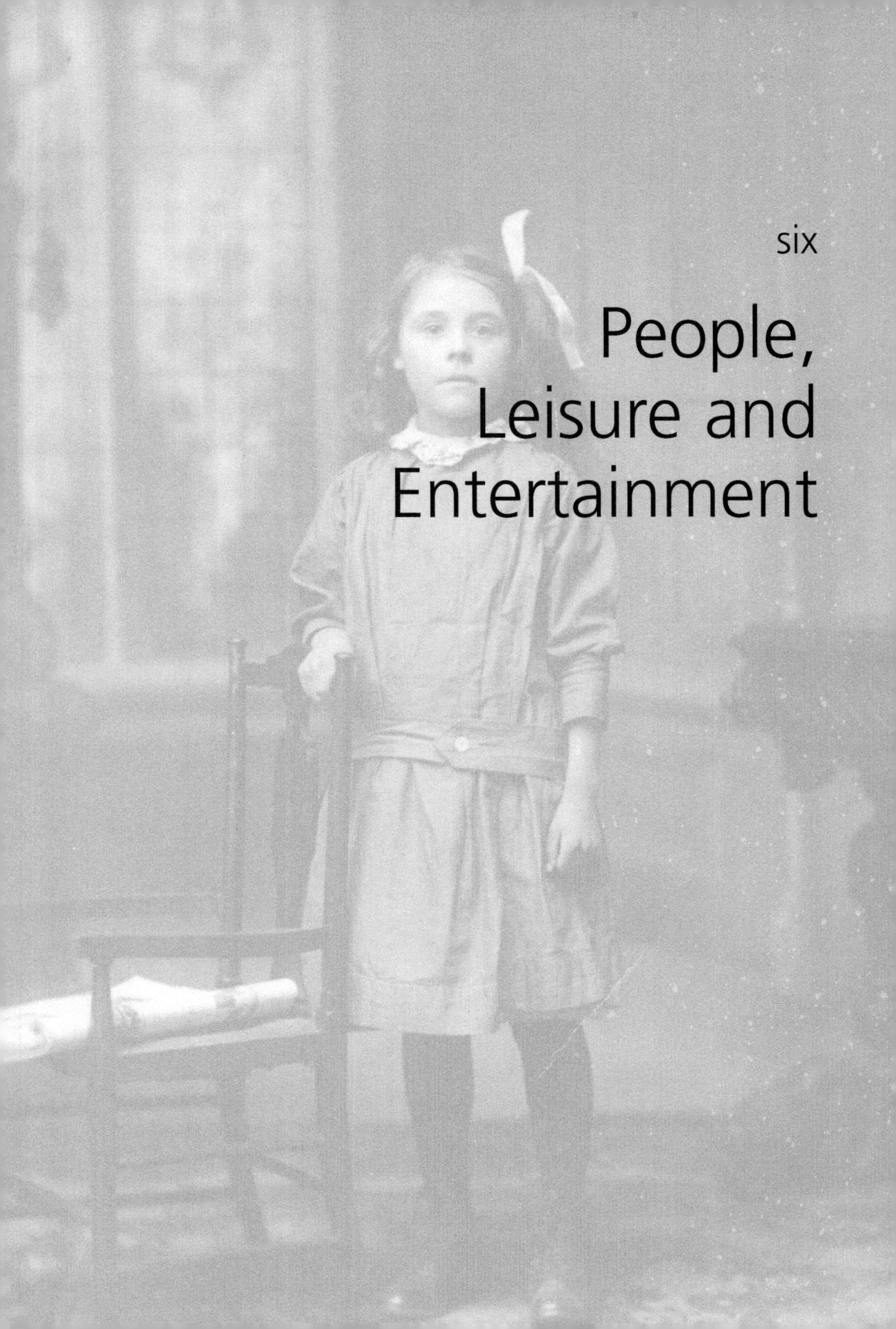

six

People, Leisure and Entertainment

William Brian was born on 29 January 1876 at No. 35 Ricardo Street, Dresden, Staffs. He became a well-known church organist in the locality and, in his teens, adopted the name Havergal which was the name of a prominent musical clergyman, William Havergal. Before long, the accomplished and talented musician Havergal Brian was being encouraged by (Sir) Edward Elgar who enjoyed his musical compositions. Brian became prolific in his works, though he died on 28 November 1972 having never heard many of his compositions – in fact, none of his music was released commercially until after his death.

Above: The family home of Havergal Brian was at No. 35 Ricardo Street, Dresden, one of the terraced properties in the middle distance of this picture. Unfortunately, there is no trace of it today since the area beyond the Park Inn up to No. 47 has been cleared and landscaped. The street was named after John Lewis Ricardo (1812-62) who was an elected Liberal Member of Parliament for Stoke-on-Trent from 1841 until his death in 1862. Ricardo was also chairman of the North Staffordshire Railway from 1846 to 1862.

Opposite: A portrait of Joan Bailey's great-grandfather Worsdale and his family dating from around 1895. Joan was brought up in the Dresden area and worked as a hairdresser in Trentham Road for many years. Her family has strong associations with the area.

Geo. W. Harker was an art photographer and picture framer. Local people would pose for formal (and informal) photographs in his studios at No. 63 Market Street. Many pictures still survive as postcards today but, unfortunately, very few are identifiable. We are all guilty of not writing on the backs of our pictures, aren't we? What is going to be available for the historians of the future to find now that we are in the age of the digital camera? How many of us catalogue our pictures once we have downloaded them onto CDs and DVDs? Do we always label the discs? This early portrait of a young girl (*c.* 1915) is completely anonymous. Presumably she is a member of a Longton family – could you be related to her?

Right: Another Harker photograph, similarly anonymous, but there are some clues on the regalia. The distinguished-looking man appears to hold high rank in the RAOB – the Royal Antediluvian Order of Buffaloes.

Below: When professional photographs were taken in studios in the early 1900s, it was usual to print them with postcard backs so they could be sent to the nearest and dearest. These would not have been made in any large quantities and could easily have been one-offs. So, it is quite common to find individual postcards bearing the name of a local photographer or publisher but for the subject to be completely unknown today. Here is a card published by Wright's IP Co. of Longton, Staffordshire, showing a man sitting at a card table with a monkey who appears to be smoking a pipe and casually revealing his hand! No names on the card so we will never know the story behind the picture – or will we?

Best Wishes
Cornetties

Opposite: Wright's seemed to specialise in publicity postcards depicting various artistes. This one shows a young couple of musicians. The card is signed, like an autograph, by 'The Cornettiers'. Extensive searching has failed to reveal anything about the publisher or the artist. Any ideas?

Right: Here is a Wright's card of a young dancer named Winnie Scaman. The surname is quite unusual and does not appear to be local to the Potteries.

Originally built as the Queen's Theatre in 1887, to a design by John Taylor, it was destroyed by fire in 1894. A new Queen's Theatre rose from the ashes in 1896, designed by the noted theatre architect Frank Matcham, and, for many years, its main role was as a variety theatre. However, it was also used to show films as part of the bill from 1911, as this new form of entertainment reached the town. In 1916 it was renamed the 'Empire Theatre' and in 1921 it finally gave way to becoming a full-time cinema. In 1966 it ceased to be a cinema and found new life as a bingo hall before finally closing its doors in 1991. After standing empty for some time the building was destroyed by a suspicious fire on New Year's Eve 1992. There were hopes that the façade could be saved but, unfortunately, all trace of this once-grand theatre finally disappeared when it was demolished in 1997.

This is a study of Sarah Bridgett when appearing in a pantomime at St Luke's, Cromartie Street. Such entertainment within church communities was commonplace in the first half of the twentieth century and brought much enjoyment to many people.

Irene Foote was born in New York, USA on 17 April 1893 and married Vernon Castle (born Blyth) in 1911. Together, they became famous for their ballroom dancing and were able to charge enormous fees giving lessons across America. They appeared in an Irving Berlin musical, *Watch Your Step*, and as themselves in *The Whirl of Life*. Irene appeared alone in the fifteen-part serialised film *Patria* under the billing of Mrs Vernon Castle. This postcard was used as an advert for the serial when it was shown at the Picturedrome on Stone Road, Longton in January 1918. Coincidentally, in the following month, Vernon Castle met his death in a flying accident whilst instructing new pilots. Irene remarried three times before her death in 1969 in Arkansas and does not appear to have made any more films.

The reverse of the postcard is overprinted with an advert for the very popular serial *Patria* starring Mrs Vernon Castle.

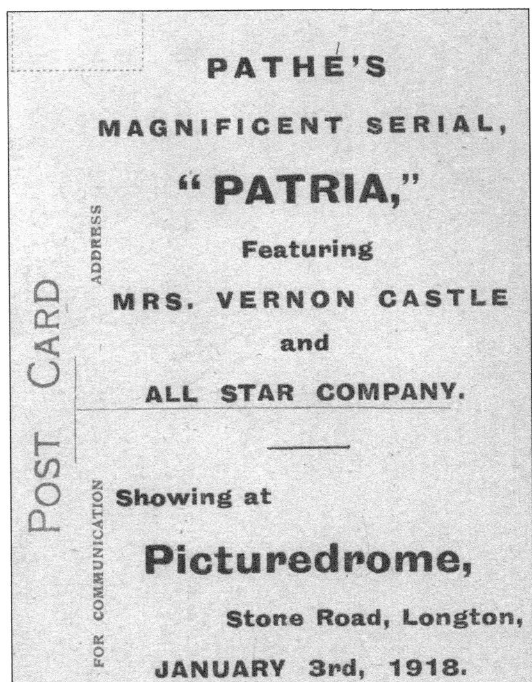

Another notable photographer in Longton was William Williamson, ably partnered by his wife Kate. Their business was started in 1914 on The Strand, at its junction with Gold Street. Since its expansion in 1931 the shop has hardly altered and to enter it today is like stepping back in time. From those early days to the present day the business of Wm. Williamson has held the commission to take the official photographs of the lord mayors of Stoke-on-Trent in their studio above the shop. In this particular portrait taken by Williamson's we see Mr Hanford Leivers (aged fifty-four) in his regalia as president of Stoke-on-Trent and District Retail Butchers' Association. Leivers' shop was next door to Williamson's on The Strand.

Bob (Robert Hanford) Leivers, born 27 December 1914 was the son of Hanford Leivers and a swimmer of distinction from an early age. He won many local and national championships and is seen here, aged 14 with some of his trophies. Throughout the 1930s, Bob Leivers, along with his friendly rival Norman Wainwright of Hanley, were Britain's leading middle distance freestyle swimmers, and both competed in the 1932 and 1936 Olympics. Bob also competed in several European and Empire Games and the highlight of his career was winning two Gold Medals and a Silver at the Empire Games of 1938. Bob followed his father's profession by becoming a butcher, but he sadly died at the age of forty-nine, having suffered from heart disease for some time.

Another studio photograph, this time on a *carte de visite* with details on the reverse showing the photographer to be John Poole of No. 216 High Street, (now Uttoxeter Road). The image would appear to date from around 1895.

These two young children are dressed in their best outfits for this early photograph by Fred Hulse, *c.* 1900. Sadly, no clues as to their identities.

J. Murray, of the Photographic Studio, No. 108 High Street, Longton, Staffordshire was responsible for this evocative snapshot. The uniformed young man stands proudly next to his (then) state-of-the-art Penny Farthing bicycle *c.* 1880. The machine is equipped with a hub-lamp and a bell which is mounted on the handle bars. From his uniform it is obvious that the young man is engaged in some formal delivery role, but as what: postman, telegram messenger or something else? According to an entry in *Kelly's Directory of Staffordshire* for 1896, Murray had moved premises by this date to Nos 11 and 15 Commerce Street and was also trading as a beer retailer! Whilst we would immediately recognise this as a Penny Farthing, in its day it was more commonly known as an 'ordinary'.

Queen's Park

Queen's Park was laid out in 1887 to commemorate Queen Victoria's Jubilee. It was the first formal park to be laid out in the Potteries and the land was presented to the town by the Duke of Sutherland. Mr John Aynsley was the driving force who organised the scheme and contributed largely to the laying out of the grounds.

This multi-view postcard gives snapshot views of the park and was on sale in around 1905 and was a popular way of communicating with friends and relatives.

This clock tower is a proud symbol of bygone benevolence and dedicated service. A plaque reads, 'The land for this park was generously given by His Grace the Duke of Sutherland KG and owing to the liberality and untiring energy of John Aynsley Esq, JP, (during his mayoralty) it was laid out and handed over to the people of Longton free from debt on the 25 July 1888. The plaque was unveiled on 6 June 1892.

Left and below: James Hilton was responsible for erecting the memorial and took the opportunity of advertising his wares on the reverse of the picture of the clock tower.

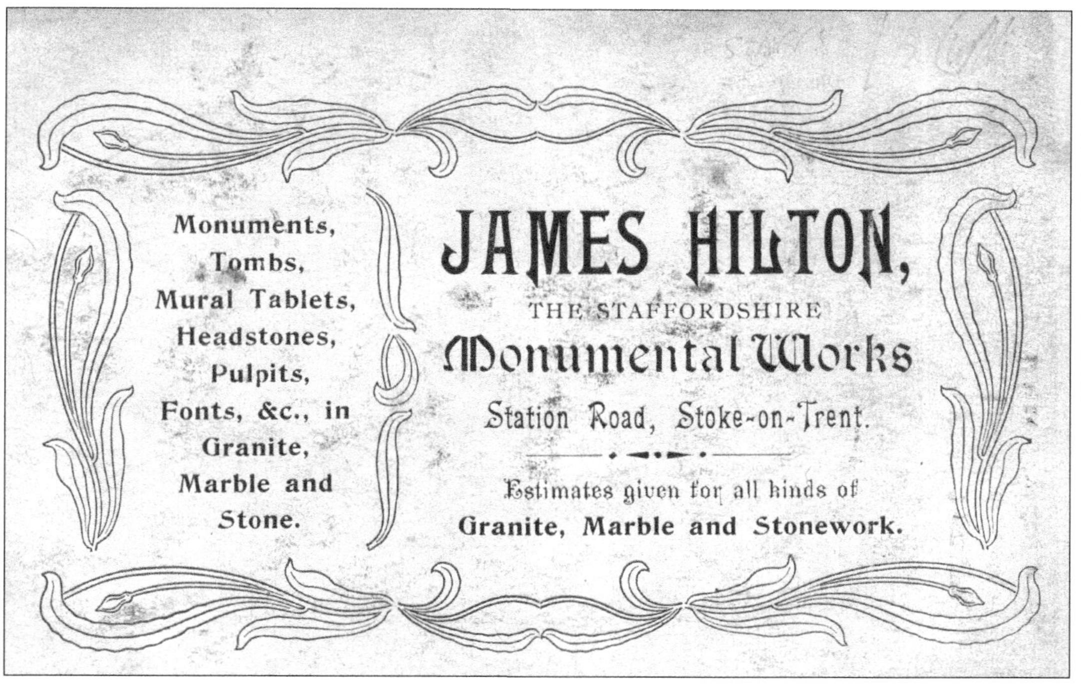

Above: In this later view of the clock tower, the trees appear much more mature and help to convey a tranquil scene.

Below: This is a splendid view which catches a glimpse of the lake to the left and leads the eye to the bowling green in the centre of the picture. Everywhere looks very lush and mature.

The bandstand area looks very lonely in this picture. You will have to use your imagination to be transported to a bygone Sunday afternoon when the band is playing and crowds are sitting around.

The park looks deserted again and the boats have been moored for the night.

What a huge slide! The children are really enjoying it. I wonder if any of them have sneaked a piece of greaseproof bread wrapper from the pantry to polish the slide and make it even faster. We didn't have to worry about Health and Safety and compensation then – least of all the council. If you fell off and grazed your knees it was all part of the fun!

That's more like it – three lads take a boat out on an adventure.

This postcard is postmarked 18 February 1905. It was sent to Miss A.E. Caulcott of Leicester and the message reads 'Dear Annie, How do you like this card? Rather pretty. Grand weather here. Just off to Stoke v Everton match. Kindest regards to all. Yours, Cyril'. Any idea what the result was? Answers on a postcard, please.

This is an early view of the lake on a postcard dated 1 August 1901.

In this picture, looking towards the houses on Queen's Park Avenue, a young mother and her baby take a rest. Let's hope that sign by the bush on the left doesn't say 'Keep Off the Grass'.

William J.B. Blake's photographs of Longton have left a wonderful record of the social life and history of the town. This picture is no exception. It is a beautiful view of the park in all its glory. There are children playing, a family on a boat on the lake and a swan making its way towards the camera.

Above: The boatman tends to his craft whilst a friend leans idly on the railings.

Below: Another view of the lake takes in the island, the boats and the boathouse. It was certainly a busy place.

Right: Another of Blake's artistic views showing a decorative flower bed and a passing swan.

Below: This postcard was published by Bloor of Longton in his E.J.B. Series. The ornate bridge was a popular subject for photographers both amateur and professional. The sign very plainly says 'Keep Off This Grass' and everyone seems to be complying. In the distance two workmen keep an eye on the photographer.

Here is granddad taking granddaughter and dog for a stroll round the park and they look pleased to pose on the bridge. The postcard was sent on 31 December 1907 with the message 'With much love and all good wishes for a joyous and prosperous New Year, from Violet'.

A couple of men rest on the bridge and keep a crafty eye on the photographer while a lone intrepid sailor circumnavigates the island.

This postcard view of the bridge has been over-printed with the words 'Season's Greetings' and was sent on 21 December 1907. Despite the sentiment, the view is quite definitely not winter…

…whereas in this view, on a postcard sent on 5 January 1907, there has quite clearly been a recent heavy snowfall.

Children play around the fountain near the entrance to the park.

A familiar sight around the streets and particularly outside the city's parks in the 1950s and '60s was the Lewis's ice-cream van, seen here on this Tuck's postcard.

94

Longton's Neighbours

LIGHTWOOD, LONGTON.

Opposite above: Travelling out of Longton
via Dresden and Florence leads to Rough
Close and then to the junction with the
A520 Stone Road. This journey passes
through Lightwood where this view was
photographed, *c.* 1910. the horse and cart is
close to the junction with Star and Garter
Road, beyond which is Gravelly Bank.

Opposite below: Another view of Lightwood
shows a pony and cart just past Gravelly
Bank heading towards Rough Close, *c.* 1904.

Right: The Bridle Path in Dresden links
Ricardo Street with Belgrave Road. Original
housing still borders the top section at
Ricardo Street but in the lower area much
of the old housing has been replaced with
modern bungalows. The tower of St James's
church on Uttoxeter Road can be seen in
the distance. The postcard bearing this view
is dated 1910, though it is possible the picture
preceded this date by a few years.

Below: It's a brave man who would drive
down the middle of Belgrave Road, Dresden,
today.

This view of Belgrave Road taken in 1912 has changed somewhat today. Whilst the chapel remains (minus its tower), the houses in the centre of the picture have gone and the road has been widened. There has also been redevelopment in the immediate area to the right.

A view of Meir Road, Normacot in 1910. The hedge on the right and the buildings opposite were removed in 1960 and recent years have seen further changes.

Tram No. 70 (introduced into service in 1900) is seen here at the terminus in Uttoxeter Road. The postcard, (in the E.J.B. series), is dated 13 November 1907. On the top of the tram an advert for Hudson's Soap is displayed.

A 1911 advert for the Sanitary Laundries Co. Ltd which were situated on Uttoxeter Road, Normacot.

Above: A view of the laundry workshop.

Left: A view of the interior of St Luke's Mission church, Cromartie Street, Florence.

Opposite above: Fenton Church of England Boys' School was opened in 1839 in Christchurch Street. The original school was built in the churchyard but a new Infants' school was erected in 1864. This class photograph is dated 1920.

Opposite below: This postcard of Fenton shows the entrance of the Royal Oak pub at the junction of High Street (now City Road) and Church Street (Christchurch Street). On the right is the junction with Manor Street where Royal Oak Furnishers have occupied the shop with the prominent corner gable for a number of years. The card was posted at 4 p.m. on 24 December 1903 with the message, 'Hope you will all have a real good time this Christmas, Yours, Geo. Barlow.' Without a doubt, the sender would have expected the card to have been delivered on Christmas Day as this was the norm at this time. Mr Barlow was a hardware dealer who traded from No. 32 Temple Street.

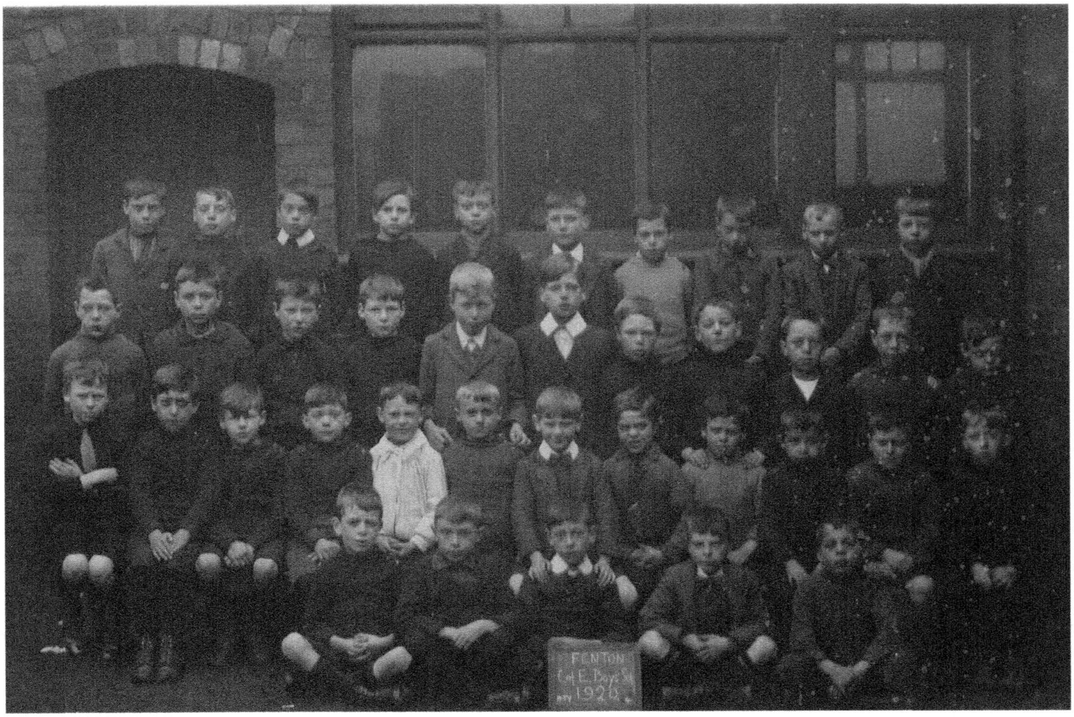

Fenton.
Staffs. High Street
Wrench Series, No. 53

A postcard of Duke Street, Fenton at its junction with Blurton Road has a chemist's shop on the corner. The message on the postcard, which was sent on 28 July 1912, reads: 'This is to let you know we have come to live at 4 Duke Street in Greengrocer's shop and father is so poorly he does not work now. Shall be pleased to see any of you if you have time. It is close to Fenton Station.'

A 1908 view of Fenton (Glebe) Collieries Ltd (1865-1964). This colliery derives its name from its association with the glebe lands of the parish church of St Peter ad Vincula, Stoke. Since its closure, the colliery spoil heap has been reclaimed and landscaped, and a mine tub and commemorative plaque have been placed on the southern side of the site to mark its association with mining.

Christ Church, Fenton, was designed by Henry Ward and built with money left in trust by Ralph Bourne. It was consecrated in 1839 but was entirely rebuilt on the same site in 1890-91 at a cost of £7,000. The tower was added in 1899 at a cost of £2,000. This view dates from 1909.

A view of the interior of Christ Church, Fenton.

Despite being in rather poor repair, this photograph of Fenton Park BC football team has survived intact for approximately 100 years. It is a very clear photograph but, sadly, there are no names or details to identify the players. Did your forefathers play for Fenton BC? Is your grandfather, great-grandfather or even great-great-grandfather in this picture?

Born around 1832, Godwin Embrey began his working life as a blacksmith, but in 1881 he appears to have changed direction and become a baker with premises in Queen Street. He also owned a second bakery at No. 29 King Street. After his death on 1 July 1890 his son, also named Godwin, continued the business which expanded. This postcard illustration of the King Street premises looks very impressive. In 1953 the business transferred to Liverpool Road, Newcastle and, by 1984, the old premises were occupied by the By-Rite showrooms.

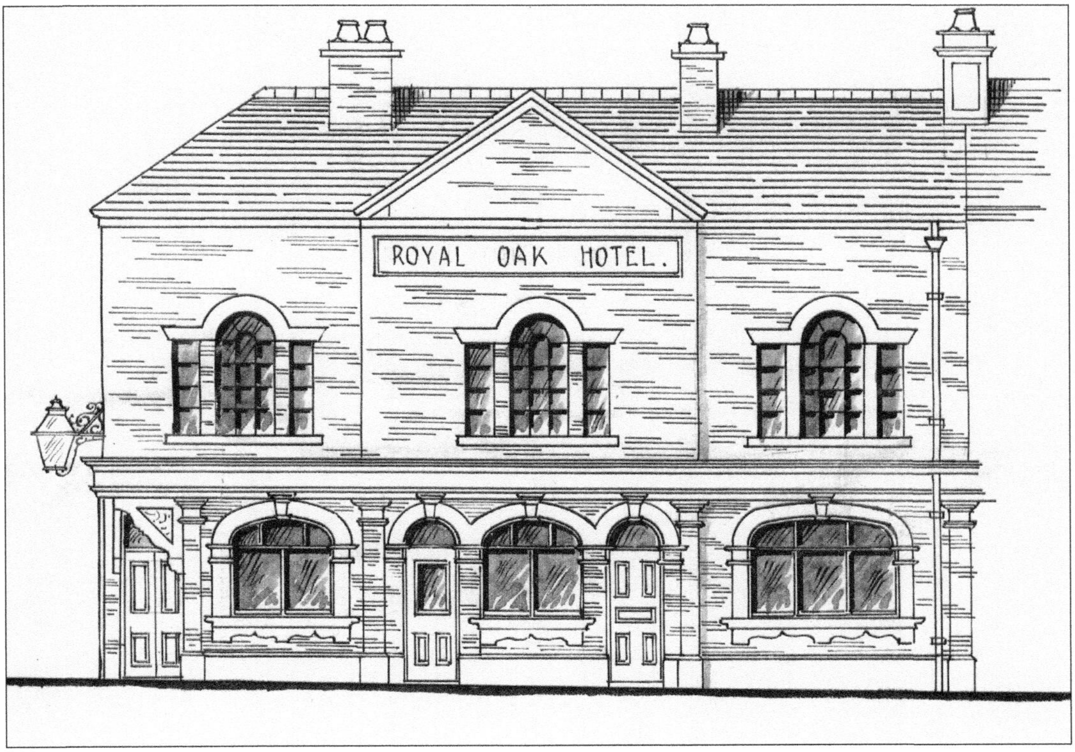

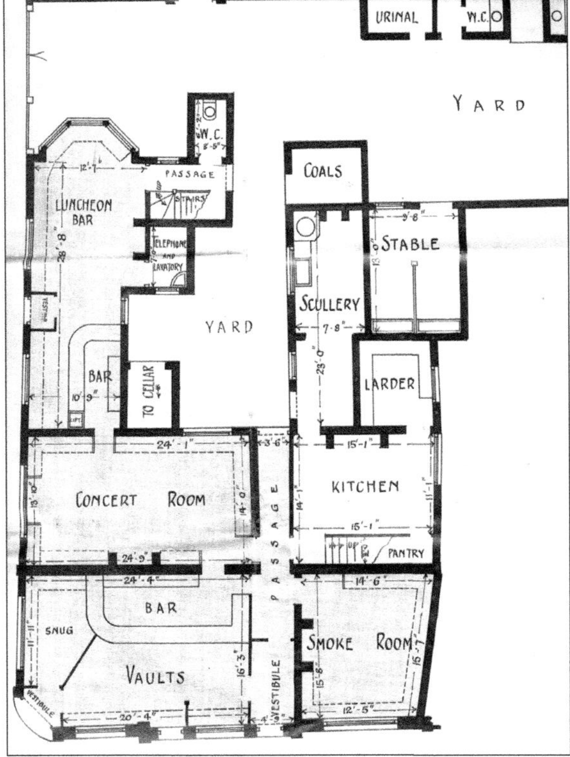

Above: This drawing of the Royal Oak at Fenton is from plans drawn up by Parker's Brewery for alterations to the public house in 1911.

Right: The ground-floor plan is from the same Parker's drawing. Note the stabling for two horses at the rear of the premises.

Heron Cross Villa FC. Back row (from left to right): T. Hodson (sec.), C. Thomas, G. Lawton, C. Tidsley, G. Nix, W. Street, T. Machin, C. Hodson (ass. sec.). Front row: A. Thomas, T. Gothan (capt.), H. Colclough, A. Spare, J. Barker, E. Hawkins (trainer). Formed about nine years earlier, this club was a member of the Tunstall Junior League. By 1935/36 the team had made its third successive appearance in the semi-finals of the Evening Sentinel Cup and went on to play in the final.

Left: The 1942 Christmas Card.

Opposite: Heron Cross Council Senior Mixed School on Grove Road was formed in 1932 following reorganisation. The buildings date from 1894 when they formed part of the buildings of Heron Cross Council School, previously the Wesleyan Day School. Thomas Lowe MBE, JP, was the headmaster when this series of Christmas cards was produced. He was obviously a very artistic amateur photographer and incorporated some innovative designs in his work. This is the 1941 School Christmas card. Were these sent to pupils and parents or sold commercially in the locality to raise funds for the school?

HERON CROSS
XMAS 1941
Greetings

Heron Cross
COUNCIL SENIOR
MIXED SCHOOL
GREETINGS

XMAS 1944
"Thomas Lowe. M.B.E., J.P. Headmaster.

Opposite: In some of the cards simple sets have been constructed to enable pupils to pose with their heads through holes made in the backdrops as can be seen in this 1944 Christmas card. In others, elaborate tableux were staged.

Right: The 1945 Christmas card.

Below: The 1946 Christmas card. By now the school had been renamed Heron Cross County Modern School.

The 1947 Christmas card.

The 1948 Christmas card.

The 1949 Christmas card.

The 1950 Christmas card. The school has been renamed again and is now known as Heron Cross
County Modern Secondary.

St Bartholomew's church, Blurton is believed to date from 1553, though its 400th anniversary was celebrated in 1977. It was enlarged in 1822 and restored in 1867, becoming a parish in its own right in 1831.

Adderley Green Colliery could trace its mining roots back to 1799, but it does not appear to have achieved significant output. Facilities in the nineteenth and twentieth centuries were poor and far from modern and, in 1935, Settle Speakman & Co. acquired the pit from its then owners Stirrup & Pye, but they closed it in 1940. This view, on a postcard dated March 1903, shows the small horse-drawn carts onto which the coal was loaded at the pithead.

This William Blake photograph shows Adderley Green Schools which stand in an elevated position close to the cutting at the top of Anchor Road. The schools date from 1884 and have undergone several extensions and changes.

A 1915 multi-view postcard of Meir.

This street party taking place in Sherwood Road, Meir is celebrating VE Day in 1945. Amongst the people enjoying the festivities are Priscilla Bath (from No. 40), with her children Gordon, Betty, Shirley, Dorothy and John. The occasion brought many friends and relatives together.

Stephen Mear & Co. was a timber merchant at No. 88 High Street, Longton and also operated as a flint and stone grinder at Anchor Mills on Goddard Street, East Vale. The mill operation passed to Mellor Mineral Mills Ltd and had ceased by the 1950s. Stephen Mear had extensive personal and business interests and was a prominent landowner. He was also a noted benefactor. Around 1890, Stephen and his brothers Alfred and James built four houses on Weston Road, Meir. This picture shows the one built for Stephen which he called Weston Coyney House. It was an extensive and substantial property reflecting Stephen's wealth, position and social standing at the time. It had tennis courts, a billiard room plus stables and pigsties. Unfortunately, Stephen's fortune was eventually lost following a disastrous court case and the Depression of the 1920s. He was later forced to realise his assets, but this was done below market value. Weston Coyney House was later demolished to make way for a small housing development. One of the remaining Mear properties became Meir Social and Sports club and the original building, similar in deign to Weston Coyney House, is now surrounded by modern extensions which have been added over many years.

View of the roundabout at Meir at the junction of Uttoxeter Road (A50) with Weston Road and Sandon Road in the 1950s. The King's Arms public house can be seen on the left.

Meir Aerodrome, initially consisting of a grass landing strip, one hangar and a clubhouse opened on 18 May 1934. This 1939 photograph shows the hangars and planes at what was then described as Stoke City Airport.

The writing on the back of this Templeman photograph reads: 'This is the plane in which Pimble took Mary Peach for a flip at Meir – then turned it over. Mary Peach walked out on the underside of the wing. Came in too low and hit fence. 1933/4.'

A tranquil rural view in Stallington Lane, Blythe Bridge, *c.* 1912.

This view of Blythe Bridge station looks along the line towards the level-crossing gates on Uttoxeter Road. The station was built on the Stoke-on-Trent to Uttoxeter line of the North Staffordshire Railway and opened in 1848.

The Weston Coyney Villas, seen here in around 1919 were built on Weston Road near to its junction with Leason Road.

Caverswall Castle was erected by Sir William de Caverswall in the reign of Edward II (1307-1327) and rebuilt by Mr Matthew Craddock during the reign of James I (1603-1625). In *Kelly's Directory* of 1896 it is described as a large mansion, with a lofty keep and towers at each angle, and it is surrounded by a deep moat. It was formerly the property and residence of a religious community of Benedictine nuns, but at this time (1896) it is the property and residence of William Eli Bowers Esq. This view of the courtyard is dated 1916.

Here are the daughters of William Eli Bowers with their ponies Bell, Pom-Pom and Tina, in 1906.

Mrs Alice Bowers in her carriage, also 1906.

Another 1906 photograph of the Bowers girls with Tina, Bell and Pom-Pom.

Above: When I said to one of the staff at Caverswall Castle, 'bring the Roller round' – this is not what I expected!

Below: St Peter's church, Caverswall is described as an ancient church whose registers date back to 1552.

Opposite: A quaint rural scene in the village of Caverswall.

Trentham Hall was the seat of the Dukes of Sutherland, lords of the manor and principal landowners in the area. In 1896 the hall was described as a mansion in the Italian style, delightfully seated on the banks of the river Trent. Sir Charles Barry was responsible for re-facing the exterior and crowning it with balustrades and vases in 1834. He also added a fine belvedere tower 100ft high. There are extensive pleasure grounds; the gardens are also extensive and laid out in the most tasteful style. There is also a deer park of over 500 acres adjacent to the hall and grounds.

The River Trent runs through the Trentham estate and, in the first few years of the twentieth century, it became heavily polluted with sewage and effluent. This also seeped into the lake and the stench became intolerable. Consequently, the hall was abandoned by the Sutherlands in 1905 and it was demolished in 1911. The gardens were opened to the public. An outdoor swimming pool was built in 1920 and a miniature railway was installed for visitors' use. This view is of the Tea Rooms and Ballroom in 1938.

The monument to the 1st Duke of Sutherland erected in the hills above Trentham in 1834 – described on this postcard as 'Tittensor Monument'.

A portrait of the Duke of Sutherland.

The Duke of York began constructing York House at St James in 1825. However, by the time of his death it remained a mere shell. It was acquired by the 2nd Marquess of Stafford (later 1st Duke of Sutherland) who completed the work on it and renamed it Stafford House. It became his London home until 1912 when it was purchased by the Lancastrian soap-maker Sir William Lever, (later 1st Viscount Leverhulme) who renamed it Lancaster House and presented it to the nation in 1913. Today, the house is used for government receptions. It lies on the edge of Green Park facing Buckingham Palace and is adjacent to Clarence House.

A picturesque scene in Spring Valley, Trentham Park.

Trentham Village looks almost deserted in this 1904 scene. Today's view is much different as the buildings
to the right have been demolished and replaced with modern housing.

A family strolls through Trentham Park past the nearby hall, *c.* 1905.

A view of the river Trent with Trentham Ballroom in the distance. After years of change and neglect the buildings have been demolished and recently replaced with a new retail area. The regeneration in recent years has been phenomenal and the area is on course to be a greater tourist attraction than ever before.

The buildings in this 1923 view of Trentham Village are no more. The black and white timbered buildings of Trentham Church of England School, dating from 1856 were due to close in 1960 and have been subsequently demolished. Apart from the strollers and the horses and carts, there is one of the area's early open-topped buses.

Other local titles published by The History Press

The South Staffordshire Coalfield

NIGEL A. CHAPMAN

Lavishly illustrated, this fascinating book relates the history of the long-gone Black Country collieries that flourished in the age of the Industrial Revolution and which did a lot to create the West Midlands that exists today.

978 07524 3102 4

Around Hanley

JOHN BOOTH

This fascinating collection of more than 180 photographs shows the people of the Potteries at work, rest and play over the last 150 years. All of the local landmarks and institutions are here, as well as the schools, churches and social clubs of this vibrant town in this nostalgic tribute to life in Hanley and the surrounding area as it used to be, 978 07524 3407 0

Tunstall

DON HENSHALL

The Staffordshire pottery town of Tunstall expanded rapidly in the nineteenth century as demand for its products grew. From factories and shops to pubs and taverns, streets, schools, churches and celebrations, every aspect of life in the area over the last two centuries is here. Compiled by local historian Don Henshall, this is a beautifully researched and wonderfully evocative tribute to life in the town as it used it be.

978 07524 3721 7

Tunstall Revisited

DON HENSHALL

This second collection of photographs from local historian Don Henshall contains rare views inside the pottery factories in their heyday, along with many familiar streets and buildings in the unfamiliar setting of yesteryear and archive images of Tunstall people enjoying their leisure time in sport and amateur dramatics or celebrating the peace at VE Day parties. It will delight anyone who has ever lived or worked in the area.

978 07524 4143 6